THE NEW ADAM

LOUIS UNTERMEYER

NEW YORK
HARCOURT, BRACE AND HOWE
1920

THE QUINN & BODEN COMPANY PRESS
RAHWAY, N. J.

A POET

(For J. S. U.)

There was a late and lonely nightingale,
That leaned its bosom on an icy thorn;
And, from the branch that threatened to impale,
A bleeding ecstasy was born.

So have you conquered agony, and torn
A triumph out of torture. Oh, rejoice
While, from the stab of loneliness and scorn,
Rises the rapture of your voice.

For the privilege of reprinting many of the poems in this volume, the author desires to thank the editors of *The Bellman, The Century, Collier's, The Dial, Everybody's, The Forum, Harper's, Good Housekeeping, The Liberator, The New Republic, The Pictorial Review, Poetry; A Magazine of Verse, Scribner's, The Seven Arts, The Smart Set, The Yale Review* and other magazines.

One of these poems originally appeared, in a slightly different version, in a previous collection of verse ("*These Times*"), and the author thanks Henry Holt and Company for permission to reprint it in its present setting.

A Note on the Poetry of Love was first published in *The New Republic.*

CONTENTS

A NOTE ON THE POETRY OF LOVE

ALMOST the first thing that strikes one after reading a quantity of Eighteenth and Nineteenth Century English Poetry is the preponderance of love-poetry. It seems to have been not only the major theme of every minor poet, it was practically the only theme of even the acknowledged leaders. Sentimental love, ideal love, platonic love, lyric and libidinous love, love elegant and *de luxe*—the variety seems all-encompassing at first glance. And then, beneath the apparent diversity of design, one is disturbed by a singular monotony; one quality stands out which gives this imposing structure a look of shoddy and crumbling artificiality. Its mass merely emphasizes its plastered columns and chipped cornices. The disillusion is bewildering. What has disintegrated? Why is it that what, in our youth, appeared to be a marble temple now seems to be little more than a suburban stucco-house?

The answer is, I believe, fairly simple. These "enamored architects of airy rhyme" were, in spite of their graceful decorations, clumsy in the use of their material; ignorant, at least as artists, of the possibilities of their most common property. They wrote endlessly of women. But, for one reason or other, women had ceased to be human to them and had become somehow both subnormal and super-terrestrial. These poets gave their mistresses strange attributes; they equipped them with inexplicable fancies and extraordinary habits of mind. Unable or unwilling to probe their differences, they accounted for them all by surrounding the opposite sex with a specious and convenient " mystery "; they made the objects of their affection less and less like ordinary human beings until their heroines seemed creatures of another and incredible world. This combination of worship and bewilderment is faithfully reflected in the inability of most modern love-lyricists to write actually about love.

Let me take, as significant examples of the same tendency, three contrary temperaments. To make the range as great as possible, let me choose Pope, Tennyson, Swinburne. To Pope, the feminine world was a world of Dresden china, polite persiflage, bonbons; a world of elaborate coiffures and compliments. Tennyson saw it as a universe of suave saints with red plush souls; his vision beheld a devotional and nun-like race dominated by impulses angelic in conception and mawkish in fulfilment. Swinburne, looking at the same world at the same time, saw it populated principally by Liliths, Faustines, Messalinas, Dolores-es, Félises, Aholibahs—a tribe of perfumed and perverse ladies lying about in Graeco-Gallic gardens. . . . None of these poets knew or, to be more accurate, knew how to express what love between the sexes really meant. To Pope it seemed a kind of fleshly *vers de société;* Tennyson found it serene and smug; to Swinburne it was sick and sensual and strange. The more these singers celebrated their heroines, the further the true figure of Woman receded until it blurred and was lost in a fog of distortion and unreality.

So—with the exception of Browning and Meredith—with all of the modern poets. Betrayed by their own preconceptions, they scarcely saw the objects of their lyrical concern. Ignoring the living model, they evolved figures exaggerated and over-colored in one-dimensional effects. Remembering only that the poetry of exaltation will be always the highest, they forgot that man's love-life is not lived on one plane, they forgot that even its exaltation is dependent on an intricacy of kindred and even contradictory moods. They forgot that all human relations, even the tenderest, have been strengthened by the commonplaces and delightful irrelevances of existence. They forgot that a fully-rounded passion has not only experienced the major emotions of possession, hate, hunger and scorn, but has also known the minor moods of irony, irritation, frivolity, *ennui*. Their poetry pretended to express the depths of the closest intimacy; it simulated candor, promised a complete exposition. But it was scarcely ever a true picture, for it omitted everything but the high lights. Even the design was false. It neglected the little fluctuating phases of love which, besides being ecstatic and mystical, are so often petulant, sportive, cynical, sometimes merely companionable, sometimes actually flippant and vulgar.

This queer combination of toughness and tenderness is not impossible in English verse.

It is not even new. It can be found not so much in the pages of the latest Georgians as in the lines of the earliest Elizabethans. What is freshest and, above all, frankest in contemporary amative verse attempts the almost forgotten blend of hardness, heat and raillery of the poets of the Sixteenth Century. A resistless curiosity quickens the literature from Marlowe to Marvell. This radiant honesty smoulders in the sonnets of Shakespeare, breaks into angry sulphur-colored flames in Drayton, showers bright sparks through the levity of Thomas Carew, plays fitfully through the mocking banter of Andrew Marvell and bursts into that blaze of grossness and awe which is the glory of John Donne.

Suddenly something went out of the world. The sparkle died; the ashes, still warm, were scattered. For almost two centuries the poetry of love was also the poetry of false postures, of attitudinizing and primping rhetoric; its very over-emphasis revealed a lack of emotional integrity. Its glow was, in the worst sense, "hard and gem-like," the sham fire of an opal; it was a celebration of the flicker not the flame. From the artificial polish of Pope to the even more polished artifice of Swinburne, little moves except in a skilfully superficial life. Real feeling gives way to a *pastiche* of emotion; in its desperate preoccupation with passion there is evident the failure to deal openly with this most difficult theme. The artist abdicates; the puritan is regnant.

It is strange that this Puritanism should be confined to the Anglo-Saxon. It is not, as one hears charged so often, a condition native to his temperament. This inhibitory reticence, incredible to the Latin or the Teuton, does not spring from a prosaic nature, for at heart the English-speaking race is essentially romantic—a tribe of adventurers, inventors, explorers; dissatisfied and probing romanticists. And yet the race that penetrated the dark heart of Africa has pirouetted before the heart of Woman and invented elaborate excuses for not exploring that darker continent. It has escaped the hazardous adventure by capitalizing Delicacy, Reverence, Womanhood. Until very recently the attitude of the English (and, for that matter, the American) amorist has been both excessively fervent and exorbitantly fatuous. When the worshiper was not prostrate in a sacramental adoration, he rose no further than his knees to an almost impossibly sentimental one. His prayers and postures were often not so much imitations of passion as parodies of it.

In the last few years we have been witnessing a return to the upright vigor, the wide and healthy curiosity of our outspoken ancestors. No longer addressing the object of man's affections as if she were an embroidered wall-motto or an abstract ecstasy, poets like Thomas Hardy, Lascelles Abercrombie, Rupert Brooke, Edwin Arlington Robinson and, most notably of all, D. H. Lawrence, are writing dramatic lyrics and monologs that reveal the loved one as fully as they express the lover. Theirs is a love-poetry that searches even while it sings. It is written with a directness that tells of a living and intimate relation. It is addressed chiefly to a woman rather than Woman, to one who is not only mistress but friend, the fellow-mortal, the divine average. It has not the sound of a perfunctory peroration or a hymn to an absent angel who has either been smirched by or cleansed of the blemish of humanity.

Such poetry combines the two urgencies which impel all vital art:—it fuses the emotion remembered in tranquillity with the passion kindled by the heat and humors of the moment.

THE NEW ADAM

THE NEW ADAM

Her body is that glorious gate
  Opening on fresh and surging skies,
The door of flesh that holds a late
  And larger Paradise.

Through this I plunge with hungry haste
  Down the old garden, stock and root.
Nothing is barred; I touch and taste
  Its unforbidden fruit.

The amorous jungle spreads its feasts,
  The lion fawns about my knee;
A new strength dawns; and all the beasts
  Are risen and contained in me.

Soft thunders gather as the glen
  Unfolds the tree from which she shakes
Her heart for me—and once again
  The wave of lightning breaks. . . .

Oh shut the gate! Let me be driven
  Down the drab byways of the past.
What right have I in such a heaven
  To whom earth clings so fast!

HANDS

Strange, how this smooth and supple joint can be
Put to so many purposes. It checks
And rears the monsters of machinery
And shapes the idle gallantries of sex.

Those hands that light the fuse and dig the trap,
Fingers that spin the earth or plunge through shame—
And yours, that lie so lightly in your lap,
Are only blood and dust—all are the same.

What mastery directs them through the world
And gives these delicate bones so great a power? . . .
You drop your head. You sleep. Your hands are curled
Loosely, like some half-opened, perfumed flower.

An hour ago they burned in mine and sent
Armies with banners charging through my veins.
Now they are cool and white; they rest content,
Curved in a smile. The mystery remains.

ASLEEP

These hands, two nimble butterflies—
  I never saw them at rest;
Nor knew a tide so regular
  Could move through your stormy breast.
You loved to meet life dancing
  With glistening steps, till all
Your fluent body seemed a curve
  In a restless waterfall.

And now you lie here so coldly,
  So unbelievably still;
A stone on a marble river,
  Ice on a wintry hill.
Something has made your beauty
  Inscrutable and grave;
Holding your once warm body
  In the curve of a frozen wave.

SUMMER STORM

We lay together in the sultry night.
A feeble light
From some invisible street-lamp crept
Into the corner where you slept;
Fingered your cheeks, flew softly round your hair,
Then dipped in the sweet valley of your breasts
And fluttered, like a bird between two nests,
Till it lay quiet there.
My eyes were closing and I may have dreamed—
At least it seemed
That you and I
Had ceased to be but were somehow
As earth and sky. . . .

The night grew closer still, and now
Heat-lightnings played between us and warm
thrills
Ran through the cool sides of the trembling hills.
Then darkness and a tension in the black
Hush like a breath held back;

A rippling through the ground, a windless breeze
That reached down to the sensitive roots of trees;
A tremor like the pulse of muffled knocks,
Or like the silent opening of locks . . .
There was a rising of unfettered seas
With great tides pulling at the stars and rocks
As though to draw them all together.
Then in a burst of blinding weather,
The lightnings flung
Long, passionate arms about the earth that clung
To her wild lover.
Suddenly above her
The whole sky tumbled in a sweeping blaze,
Gathering earth in one tight-locked embrace,
Drenching her in a flood of silver flame.
Hot thunders came;
And still the storm kept plunging, seeking ever
The furthest cranny, till the faraway
Streams felt each penetrating quiver
And the most hidden river
Rose and became released. . . .

At last the stabbings ceased,
The thunders died.

But still they lay
Side by side,
While moonbeams crept
Into the heavenly corner where earth slept;
Dipping among her rosy hills, lighting above
Her curved and sloping hollows, till
She too was still.
Beloved and blest,
His cloudy head lay, seeking rest
In the sweet-smelling valley of her breast,
And each was huddled in each other's love;
Or so it seemed . . .
My eyes were closing and I may have dreamed.

WALLS AGAINST EDEN

Now Adam, dazzled, ill at ease,
  Inspects the copper-colored skies;
Ringed with the roar of strange machineries,
  He thinks of Paradise.

Yes, this is better. Here, at least,
  Is speed and struggle, not the old
Languor of Eden and the lukewarm beast—
  Here life is hot and cold!

Released for action, Adam is
  God in these swift complexities;
He laughs and leaps from cliff to precipice,
  Lurches through toppling seas.

New grain is always his to thresh,
  Through him all energy is hurled;
He rides triumphant on the tides of flesh,
  Pride of a gaping world.

Yet Adam, hero of all he sees,
  Remains untamed, unreconciled;
And, in the midst of swaggering victories,
  Turns like a wayward child;

Hungers for all he spurned, and shrinks
  From clamor and the applauding cries;
Lost in a storm of dreams, he sinks
  Remembering Paradise.

A MARRIAGE

I tell you it is over and I mean it.
  You have been tugging at my joy too long.
The coming of the end—you must have seen it—
  Finds us still struggling, stubborn but not
    strong.

You light your darkness on me, you rekindle
  Things long burnt out upon my warmth in vain.
Your flicker fails; the gusty fires dwindle.
  And though you use me up, what do you gain?

If you could only drink some buoyance from me
  Or draw me up, like blood, to be transfused.
But all your heavy broodings overcome me,
  And leave us both bewildered and misused.

Well, let us try once more this magnifier
  Of pride and passions. Let it burn us through.
Come, take of me whatever you require;
  I shall not tell you what I steal from you.

Thus, feeding but not fed, we waste each other,
And war with weapons never understood;
And win, with each new ending, one another;
And take up arms again . . . and find it good.

WRANGLE

The room was tense with a sullen silence;
There was no sound
But the tentative chirping of a caged canary.
Suddenly you said, ". . . . ."

And there were only
Your words and mine,
Beating their two-edged swords,
Clashing and wounding with a fierce intolerance;
Seeking the belovèd blood.
Red and smoking words,
Hurling their brands in a dark abandon.
Words of destruction,
Hot to the hand,
Hotter to the throat;
Words of living, hurtling steel,
Blazing, bursting, screaming, shattering. . . .

Till there remained nothing
But the caged canary,
Pouring his cool passion
Over the glowing ruins of our peace.

NEUROSIS

Can this be you, this harsh, contemptuous thing;
  Loveless and loathsome? Will you never shed
This angry hatred? Must you turn and sting
  Whatever you can hurt, discomfited?

Now it is two o'clock. We both have tired
  Beneath the blows of futile argument.
And still you rouse yourself to strike, inspired
  With some dark force that never can be spent.

You will have one thing only and no other,
  And even that seems hopeless and defiled.
You who have forced yourself to be my mother,
  Resent the fact that you are not my child.

Alone in this, your baffled insurrection,
  You will not arbitrate although you fall;
Facing a world of blundering imperfection,
  Blind to its offers, you reject them all.

I see you, torn and lashed by your frustration,
  Turning to rend what little joy you find;
In love with nothing more than cold negation,
  You seek but never hope to meet your kind.

How will this suicide of fierce denial,
  This rivalry of light and darkness end?
Will you not give yourself a desperate trial
  And, much forgetting, learn to comprehend
  Love that is less a father than a friend?

THE WANDERER

Is it a tribute or betrayal when,
  Turning from all the sweet, accustomed ways,
I leave your lips and eyes to seek you in
      Some other face?

Why am I searching after what I have?
  And going far to find the near at hand?
I do not know. I only know I crave
      To find you at the end.

I only know that love has many a hearth,
  That hunger has an endless path to roam,
That beauty is the ghost that haunts the earth
      And leads me home.

INFIDELITY

You have not conquered me; it is the surge
Of love itself that beats against my will;
It is the sting of conflict, the old urge
That calls me still.

It is not you I love, it is the form
And shadow of all lovers who have died
That gives you all the freshness of a warm
And unfamiliar bride.

It is your name I breathe, your hands I seek;
It will be you when you are gone.
And yet the dream, the name I cannot speak
Is that that lures me on.

It is the golden summons, the bright wave
Of banners calling me anew;
It is all passion, perilous and grave—
It is not you.

PICNIC ON THE GRASS

You, with your face to the sky,
  Here, but still out of my reach,
Listening gravely while I
  Burst into passionate speech.

Begging you not to delay,
  While youth is a jubilant strife,
Till your hair turns a virtuous gray
  And your grandchildren mock you with life.

Saying, "You must not deny,
  But burn yourself out with the flame;
This placidly living a lie
  Is ten times as shameful as shame.

"Oh, rouse yourself; kindle and burn
  With April before it slips" . . .
You move your head slightly and turn
  Your whimsical eyes to my lips.

Your eyes seem to lift with a queer
  Light, as of battle half-won;
They challenge, " Come, make yourself clear,
  O wise man." And I—I talk on.

DUST

Listen—the dust at our feet whispers and breathes.
It speaks in a voiceless air that is delicate but august.
Hurry, it says, for the wave that rushes and seethes
Will spend itself on the rocks and crumble with you in the dust.

I turn from the earth to your eyes; they are bright as before.
Your ears can hear nothing grave. That is merciful and just.
Thank God that you are not burdened with knowledge and useless lore;
You can dance through a world that surrenders to murder, to squalor and lust.

Thank God, your eyes are screened from the day that I see
When your laugh is a bony grimace and the gold in your hair is rust;
When your flowery hand, with its five white petals, will be
A sensitive flower, turned yellow, that withers and droops in the dust. . . .

And we will be lying apart, but compassionate winds will blow,
Mingling our little separateness, a handful of doubt and distrust.
And the years will come thundering by; triumphantly they will go
To creep back broken and join us, with the night, in the frail dust.

COME!

Once more you falter and delay;
Your feeble courage fails again.
You'll yield to me, sometime, you say.
When?

When will you make all this worth while,
And put our jangling world in tune?
You answer, with a frightened smile,
"Soon."

But soon I will be cold and dumb
To your warm lips and child-like brow.
Faint heart, hold off no longer. Come—
Now!

EQUALS

You child, how can you dare complain
  That you and I may be mismated
Because, you say, you lack a brain
  And I'm so highly educated.

The body is the greater thing;
  And you are doubly gifted when
You have such hands and breasts that bring
  More peace than all the plans of men.

Take pride in this, your beauty; drink
  The wine it offers for our love.
Be glad you do not have to think—
  One thoughtful lover is enough!

Holding the dearest things too cheap,
  You give yourself a needless strife;
Wiser than words, your dumb limbs keep
  More secrets than I know of life.

We're equal partners, that is plain.
  Our love cannot grow dull or shoddy
While I have such a lively brain
  And you have such a lovely body.

LOVE

You close your book and put it down,
As one might drop a tiresome task;
And, with what tries to be a frown,
You turn and ask:

" How can you care one hour for me
Unless your love is all a sham?
' Childish and cheap '—but can I be
More than I am?

" Your poet knows that love delights
Only its equals, near or far . . .
' *We love the things we love,*' he writes,
' *For what they are.*' "

You serious child, how can you place
Such utter credence in a song?
It is, I grant, a lovely phrase;
But it is wrong.

Why look, my darling, at the world
  Rolling in blood and murderous flame.
And what's this life? A brief torch hurled
    To darkness, whence it came.

The world is easy to revile
  Where much is false and little true.
And yet we live in it, and smile.
    —And love it, too.

Cease, then, to talk of wrong or right;
  Finalities are cold and far.
We love the things we love in spite
    Of what they are.

IVORY AND ROSE

Here in this moonlit room, I watch you slip
  One shoulder from your dress and turn to me;
A polished statue, flushing to the tip
  Of marble fingers gradually.

And, like a ripe moon out of flimsy clouds,
  Blossoms the shining fullness of your breast.
These curves conceal, this dear perfection shrouds
  A soft, miraculous nest.

Your ivory body pulses as the white
  Flesh catches flame and rosy tremblings move
Over this sanctuary of delight,
  The last asylum of our love.

HAIR-DRESSING

Before the prim, old mirror
  That stands so stiffly there,
With puritan precision
  You re-arrange your hair.

Knitting your childlike forehead,
  As, with a whimsical pout,
Your fingers, smooth and dextrous,
  Bring order out of rout.

But here a coil escapes you,
  And there a bright strand shakes
Over your neck and shoulders,
  Like little, yellow snakes.

Serious and ensnaring,
  Each skillful hand begins
To make a knotted pattern,
  Bristling with puffs and pins.

You pause to turn and ask me
  How this appears, or that,
Till all is smoothed and finished
  With a last, loving pat. . . .

My pretty, proper darling,
  With not one hair amiss,
Who turns, like some calm duty,
  One powdered cheek to kiss,

Are you the same wild creature
  I held last night, and found
Sleeping upon my shoulder
  With all her hair unbound?

SUPPLICATION

Take away your soft hair and your softer lips,
Loose me from your twining fingers; turn away your eyes.
For I loved this earth, and now a headlong passion slips
All its earthly ties.

I can wait for heaven, if that is to be;
Let me have those common days and know their simple worth.
Do not make the quiet-colored moments dull to me—
Let me keep the earth.

There is much I long to look at, much I long to taste.
You have mocked a thousand raptures with contemptuous power.
Do not let your beauty lay all other beauty waste;
Spare a casual hour.

Let old music thrill me to my finger tips;
Bring me back the glamor of the things I used to prize;
Lift this cloudy radiance where I only see your lips.
Turn away your eyes!

WORDS

Why are your lips so soft and still?
    They neither laugh nor weep.
Scorn cannot rouse, nor anger kill
    The silence that they keep.

Your quiet drowns my vehemence
    Till I grow hard and seek
A harsher tone, a loud offence
    To make you start and speak.

But when I see those silent lips
    Tremble like startled birds,
I put away the cowardly whips
    Snapped by my lashing words.

And when they cling to mine, they reach
    Beyond the sphere of sense;
They put to shame my deafening speech
    With love's dumb eloquence.

THE MOON

What cold, celestial laughter
  Disturbs me in the night?
It is the moon that enters
  The street with a ripple of light.

His ghostly mirth reminds me
  How well I ought to know
That flash of evil humor
  Revealed some months ago. . . .

Upon a beach where the pattering
  Waves were music enough
Two lovers walked, believing
  The world was made for their love.

The stars, the crooning silence
  Worked through their stammering lips;
Slowly it drew them together
  Like rudderless, driven ships.

In the deserted pavilion
  They clung with a passionate faith;
Hurling, as though for the first time,
  The deathless challenge to death.

. . . .

And then, old moon, I saw you.
  Your sharp and cynical smile
Cut through our boasts and bravados,
  Breaking them off for a while.

Your long, ironic glances
  Mocked us and seemed to inquire,
What ash would be left tomorrow
  Of this brief spasm of fire?

We paused. And then, for an answer,
  She laughed in my arms and said,
" Why should the living listen
  To you, the impotent dead! "

INTERCESSION

Night,
Take down the moon's keen sickle
And reap a bright
Destruction on these light and fickle
Souls that dance with every wind.
Sweep left and right
Until these overplanted fields are thinned.
But spare
In your intolerant wrath,
One flower struggling where the path
Is overgrown with weeds and grass.
The rain has barely touched her thirst.
Let her drink sunlight first.
Night, when you see her waiting there,
Pass.

LAST WISHES

Not mine alone and never wholly mine
Can your heart be;
I share you with a jealous world,
With children, stars, a tree.

And with what quick and generous recompense
They turn to you.
You give them love: they give you love
And tributes, too.

You seem to cling to me, but they alone
Will hold you fast.
Each look you give them is as long
As though it were your last.

Such love should be my living monument:
Let others see
In your unconquerable delight
How you delighted me.

ENOUGH

If we have nothing more now,
    We have had this:
The keen joy of our bodies,
    The white, unearthly bliss

Of peace beyond all passion,
    Beyond all pain;
Tears which have healed the wounds that
    We opened time and again;

Days, when each casual greeting
    Was a new thrill;
Nights, when love touched and took us
    Almost against our will;

Hours of beauty and banter—
    A cry and a kiss . . .
Let the earth crumble beneath us.
    We have had this!

THE MATCH

Do you recall our first few moments together,
Or do you forget?
You stammered and said something vague about the weather;
I offered a cigarette

And took one for myself, and there were snatches
Of laughter as you tried
To keep aflame those weak, half-hearted matches
That flashed and died.

Finally, with an effort, you succeeded;
And, shielding it with your hand,
You offered me the only spark I needed.
You did not understand

When, as I leaned to you and the flame leaped higher
And you would not let it go,
I warned you, laughing, you were playing with fire . . .
Now you know!

THE BEREAVED

Rich in your grief, I watch you go
Wearing the perfume and the pomp of woe;
Deprived of nothing half so much
As of the things you will not see or touch.
Your pale and half-transparent thought
Is, even in its simple strictures, caught
By all the platitudes of pride
And self-indulgence that you cannot hide.
You have bereaved yourself of many things
Besides the bird-like, childish joy that sings
Within your spirit, that which loves
Whatever runs and leaps or merely moves.

Forget this self-inflicted hurt
And find yourself in all the sharp, alert
Business of living. Join once more
The human stream that surges past your door.
Go, leave your dead and live again
In the miraculous, laughing world of men.
See how this shop-girl's hunger thrills
With romance walking on the painted hills;

Or watch her dull and wooden boy
Burn with a hungrier fire than levelled Troy.
For you a thousand points of light
Pierce through the funeral draperies of night;
The dead years scorn their cenotaph
And in your blood all ages leap and laugh.
For you the sun goes riding by
Over the flaming ridges of the sky,
And every swift, adventuring day
Jeers at your dark, ridiculous display.
Let these things have you till you grow
Ashamed of your denial, and you go,
Shedding your truant airs, like one
Who finds instead of death and life undone,
Only the promise of a thing begun.

MATTER

When I was a live man
    A few years ago,
For all I might say,
    For all I could do.

I got no attention;
    My life was so small
The world didn't know
    I was living at all.

Such stolid indifference
    I couldn't allow;
I swore that I'd matter—
    Never mind how.

But after a lifetime
    Of hunger and prayer,
I broke my heart trying
    To make the world care.

And now as I lie here,
　　Feeding this tree,
I am more to the world
　　Than it is to me.

FANTASY

A bird ran up the onyx steps of night,
  Seeking the moon upon her silver throne;
But stars confused him with their insolent light
  And left him in the friendless skies, alone.

He watched the winds, disheveled and awry,
  Hurling the clouds, like pillows from their
    beds;
He saw the mountain-peaks that nudged the sky,
  Take off the wreaths of sunset from their heads.

He heard the storms, a troupe of headstrong boys,
  Locked up as punishment for petulant tears,
Beat on the ebony doors with such a noise,
  That all the angels had to hold their ears.

Frightened, he left the halls of thundering sound
  For a less dazzling height, a lowlier dream;
And, perching on a watery bough, he found
  The moon, her white laugh rippling from the
    stream.

MATINÉE

The poet stood reciting
  Examples of his art,
Considerately removing
  The veils about his heart.

Eager and self-revealing,
  He did his stripping well;
With every burning poem
  Another garment fell.

With passionate abandon
  He flung each cloth away;
Exulting in the pleasure
  Of noble self-display.

Until upon the platform
  Were piled his draperies.
And still the poet gestured,
  Naked and quite at ease.

And no one screamed or fainted;
  There was no stir or start.
The ladies all applauded
  Such a display of Art.

THE ETERNAL MASCULINE

Woman, though you never heed me,
  Though our ways are seldom one,
Still I look for you to lead me
      Up and on.

Be my lamp, my steadfast beacon;
  Be my friend, philosopher;
And, if I should halt or weaken,
      Be my spur.

Draw me onward; leave me burning;
  Lash my thoughts with beauty's thong.
Have no pity while my yearning
      Makes me strong.

Let me seek you out, but fly me;
  Never drop the luring mask.
Teach your mercy to deny me
      All I ask.

Still your spirit's superhuman
Power calls the best in me . . .
Therefore, warm and earthly Woman,
Let me be.

ANNA

There's that you've not attempted;
There's that you could not be;
But these things are forgiven you—
At least by me.

Others are brighter, braver;
Others more sweetly-grown;
But you've a salt and savor
Of your own.

Earthy and hard and wholesome,
You stand here, golden-faced;
Fresh as a young nasturtium—
And sharper to the taste.

NOCTURNE

What was that so hidden
  In your guarded mirth,
When the veils of purple moonlight
  Screened the timid earth?

When impetuous April
  Called its reticent bride,
What was in your laughter
  That you could not hide? . . .

Now a bird's note rises,
  Colorless and cool,
Like a spray of silver bubbles
  From a snowy pool.

And you smile, a warmer
  Mystery than the bird's.
Come, reveal the music—
  Never mind the words.

LANGUAGE

On the soft heaven of your breast,
  My worn-out body lies;
Infinite solace, infinite rest
  Lift me through opening skies.

Beyond myself, toward some far goal,
  I mount, peak after peak;
Great waves of music wash my soul.
  And then—you start to speak.

Swiftly the calm and casual word
  Severs us each from each;
The earth springs back with your absurd
  Relapse to empty speech.

I tumble down from heaven and clutch
  At stars my fingers miss.
O close your lips; they move too much
  Save when they move to kiss.

Be still, I tell you. Let us lie
  And feel Love's silent growth.
O, never speak at all, for I
  Can talk enough for both!

CATALOGUE

Why all these fears and feigned alarms
  That never can pretend to blind me?
Let me enumerate the charms
    With which you bind me.

First, I shall list one pair of eyes,
  Like flame beneath some smouldering fuel;
A mouth that's witty if not wise,
    Half kind, half cruel.

Thirdly, there are two tapering hands,
  So delicate and diamond-spangled;
And there's your hair, in whose bright strands
    I lie entangled.

Your breast, all rose and silk and pearl;
  Your laugh, a bright and sharpened sickle;
Your whims, dear and distracting girl,
    Footloose and fickle.

Your kiss, a wine that has no dregs;
  Your love, a bird that seldom perches.
And I must add your lyric legs—
    Two dancing birches.

But most of all I love your pride,
  As firm as mine that I believe in.
Stubborn and selfish; hard inside . . .
    That makes us even.

"SO REIN UND SCHÖN"

(*With a volume of Heine*)

Like some young flower, cool and white,
  With the stars' kiss still on its brow,
You shine through my heart's dusk, and light
  The dark concern that gathers now.

Half on my lips, a fearful hope
  Starts like a prayer, already planned.
Toward your bright head my fingers grope . . .
  But something holds my hand.

Prayers are not what you want. I see
  That, when all other beauty fails,
You will not alter, you will be
  So white and young—and hard as nails.

RAPUNZEL

Let down your hair,
  That cloudy-gold lure,
The delicate snare
  That holds me secure.
Delight and despair
  War with me now—
Let down your hair.

Shake out each curl
  Swiftly, and be
Like Spring, a wild girl
  With her hair flying free.
Bury me there,
  And be buried with me . . .
Let down your hair!

WINDY DAYS

The red wind tears and the bright leaves are
    hurled
Down to their death. A rain of crimson spots
The rusty-colored earth; the young fruit rots,
Killed by the fiery gusts that sweep the world.
There is a treacherous poison in the year
That withers every branch and delicate fern;
Even the cloudy heavens smoke and burn . . .
And what, belovèd, are we doing here?

There's no escape; this tiny stretch of park
Echoes the clash and thunder of the town.
We cannot lose the world; it tracks us down
And spreads its wars till even peace grows dark,
Here where no bird dares lift a frightened wing
To try new heights or find a place to sing.

BRAIN AND HEART

What fertile and malignant plan
  To flood the world with greater pain,
Could so desire to torture man
  By giving him a heart and brain.

Crippled with these, he cannot be
  A beast, a basker in the sun,
A growing pleasure like a tree,
  But he must cower, cringe and run

Before the winds of memories
  That rumble with his childhood's fears;
A handful of hypocrisies
  Still sends him reeling through the years.

Poor worms that die upon a crust,
  Betrayed and bitten by a dream,
Maggots that yield to every lust
  With a deific self-esteem;

Driven by every twist of thought
  Beyond their pitiful desires—
In what net are these creatures caught;
  Plunged in what self-enkindled fires?

If there's one god who sees a part
  Of all men's burdens—old or new—
He'll take away this brain and heart
  And let the poor things muddle through.

MOZART

How calmly this beauty falls,
Confident, careless and futile;
Like rain upon troubled waters
Or stars on a field of battle.

The night, this music, these times
And you are clashing within me.
I am bruised and broken with visions,
A dark wood where sunlight is splintered.

BEYOND SOUND

The poets cry, the preachers drone
  Of glories that are never heard.
And yet the moon, a worn white stone,
  Says all they say without a word.

Their praise is loud, they smite the air
  With eloquent and clashing zeal;
They force their love, while they declare
  'Tis only half of what they feel.

Their thundering speech is quickly done;
  Hushed by the deathless hymn that flows
From the mute passion of the sun,
  The burning silence of a rose.

CONFIDENCE

Supposing the night should roar
  Like a great beast unchained,
And the river in front of my door
  Should rise with a rending voice;
Though all the leaves of the oak
  In a gust of derision were rained,
And the winds should tramp till they broke
  All things that dance or rejoice—

Still I would smile and have peace
  Though the passionless stars should go mad;
Knowing this frenzy must cease
  And quiet will sing to me soon.
I know that a silent laughter
  Will comfort me when I am clad
In the golden indifference of sunlight
  And the silver scorn of the moon.

DISTANCES

I read your note, and with it comes
  A feverish expectancy;
It stirs my blood as though great drums
  Were calling out in me.

Out of the struggling lines, a hand
  Gropes and your large eyes make me start;
You mock at space, although we stand
  A hundred miles apart.

Yet when we two come face to face,
  I have a different sense of loss;
Somewhere, there is a widening space
  We cannot hope to cross.

The distance grows, it stretches far,
  Even when we lie heart to heart.
You hold me close—and yet we are
  Ten thousand miles apart!

ALMOST

My sweetheart has beneficent arms
  So full of tenderness and fire,
They almost cheat her other charms
  The way they rouse and still desire.

My sweetheart has the kindest breast,
  Two heavens with each a single star;
They give me everything but rest,
  So strange these rosy pillows are.

My sweetheart has the hungriest lips
  That seek and press unsparingly;
They probe until she almost slips
  Among her kisses into me.

My sweetheart's body is a cry,
  A poignant and resistless call;
It almost makes me wonder why
  She hasn't any mind at all.

HOMAGE

Now that I've won you, you complain
  I have forgotten how to woo you.
My words, you say, have lost the strain
  That drove the young blood singing through
      you.

No longer do I celebrate
  " Your hair that shames the fire of Titian ";
Nor swear, " Your beauty is so great
  That it would check a god's ambition."

I have forgotten how to play
  The nimble echo, nimbler servant.
But I do homage in a way
  That is less facile but more fervent.

I worship as a mortal can;
  And something more than words must show it.
I love you too much as a man
  To want to love you as a poet!

THE EMBARRASSED AMORIST

I cannot choose between them now,
  And yet I have to choose.
A hand, a foot, a child-like brow,
  Enrapture me. . . . But whose?

I seem to have no will at all,
  Only a stubborn need;
Blindly I follow beauty's call
  Wherever it may lead.

I run to Anna's soothing arms,
  Knowing that peace is best—
And then the thought of Lucy's charms
  Provokes me out of rest.

I tear myself, but I am loath
  To tear my soft chains free.
How can I strike at one, when both
  Seem so wrapped up in me?

And though I know what should be done,
I know what I cannot do. . . .
It's heaven to be in love with one
But hell to be loved by two!

THE VOICE

I cannot recall your features,
  Your words I scarcely caught;
But I shall always remember
  The vision that they brought:—

Blue depths and a cool air ruffling
  The silver tops of trees;
A thousand young stars dancing
  Down dark, adventurous seas.

Voices of children and heroes;
  The moon on the crest of a wave;
A challenge of golden trumpets
  Over a restless grave.

A STREET WALKER

Four times she has passed this place,
  Seeking a lover or food;
With what was a childlike face
  Turned hardened and shrewd.

Her eyes looked left and right
  With scarcely a turn of the head;
They were glassy and far too bright
  Like the eyes of the dead.

The glare of the arclight strips
  Her glamour and feeble pretense;
The smile on those shrunken lips
  Would make a man wince.

Yet, in those terrible eyes
  And in that gesture, I see
A poignance that struggles and cries
  Directly to me.

The failure, the baffled grace
  Is something I somehow knew.
That hard, little, pitiful face—
  It might have been you.

THE DERELICT

She drifts by under the lights,
  Flaunting her tattered sails;
Wreck of a thousand nights
    And a thousand gales.

A derelict, yet she trades
  With an ensign that's never furled;
An outcast, though she parades
    The flags of the world.

Washed by the tides of unrest,
  Chartless, but never free,
She floats on the passionate breast
    Of a passionless sea.

IMPLICATION

God, you complain, gave you a pretty face—
  And that, you half imply, explains it all;
  Your sudden rise and still more sudden fall;
The flashy triumph and half-proud disgrace.
Bitter, but still resolved to keep your place,
  You mock at signs of faith and honor, call
  Life an unmeaning farce, a madman's brawl,
And lay it all on Him, in any case.

But why blame God? Is it His fault again?
  He knows, it seems, little of needs or goals;
God's a haphazard giver, and all men
  Grow careless with their battered aureoles.
He made you with a pretty face. . . . But then,
  God can not make us all with pretty souls.

TECHNIQUE

So that's to be your tale? But who'll
Believe you?
What sort of mad, incredible fool
Could so deceive you?

One could as easily betray,
I warrant,
A lioness or, full of play,
Seduce a torrent.

You charge your anguish with a rough
Bravado . . .
But is one always carried off
By a tornado?

"Wronged! Wronged!" you trumpet. "Led astray!"
You shout it.
Vengeance? But really, that's no way
To go about it.

Too loud for sympathy, and still
        Too pretty,
Your robust protestations kill
        Our faltering pity.

The crushed and half-bewildered air
        Is better.
With this, you'll find a host to wear
        The tightening fetter.

A drooping pathos that is frail
        But quiet . . .
And, when you're wronged again, turn pale,
        And gulp—and try it.

GHOSTS

The long street blares, the arclight throws
  A singing halo 'round your head;
And yet, in spite of all that glows,
  This is a city of the dead.

Dead, they are dead, these folk who run
  Through pleasure in such darkening hosts;
While the old moon, a long dead sun,
  Grins at this cavalcade of ghosts.

Dead, they are dead to every spark
  Of struggling beauty, passionate aim;
Touched by some fire in the dark,
  They smoulder but they cannot flame.

They are too dead to burn; too damp
  With mouldy thoughts and rotting peace;
Life is to them a low-turned lamp
  Lighting them to a bed of ease.

This masque of faces, dull and bland—
  Are these the tribes that bore and bled?
You smile. . . . You do not understand.
  Good God! Can even you be dead!

THE SHRINE

Beautiful, wise—but you do not compel
  Worship beyond a bent and willing knee;
Your loveliness is a familiar bell
    Ringing incessantly.

Yours is a dazzling and unblemished shrine;
  The niches burn with color, candles sing.
Yet bread is bread, and water is not wine
    For all your murmuring.

Yes, you are like a splendid house of prayer,
  A sanctuary where no joy has trod;
But I can never stand in reverence there
  Where there are lights and altars—but no god.

ADVICE

And do you truly feel surprise
That I no longer idolize;
That I who seemed to bow and pray
Have smashed my gods and run away.
You cannot think how much it pains
To slip the ineffectual chains;
But many others, you'll agree,
Will wear them far more gracefully.
So dry those forced, infrequent tears—
Emotion always interferes
With the manipulated grace
Of your *svelte* hands and chiselled face.
It takes a special sort of art
To simulate a broken heart,
And you should never try to act
A part where fancy turns to fact.
Always you should maintain that air
Of hushed and delicate despair;
The mood of great things to suppress
That you first wore with such success.

Never should you attempt again
The rôle of the tragedienne,
The worn-out rant that tries to show
A passion you can never know.
Be cool or dutiful or dense,
But never try to be intense.

Your other lures were swift and strong.
You caught me in the snares of song;
You put soft fetters on my feet;
But—ere your mastery was complete—
You tried for greater power: you sought
To charm me in the realms of thought.
Oh self-deluded girl, what vain
Pride made you dare that dark domain.
Trying to rule in that strange land,
The sceptre trembled in your hand.
It fell. You tottered; clung to me;
Then, growing frightened, set me free.

My dear, you should have been content
With a more lenient government;
You should have let your beauty go
Down the light roadsides that you know.

Playing an inconspicuous part,
You would have held me, hand and heart.
But no—you thought that you could bind
My fetterless and scornful mind.

Farewell . . . Why, you look half-resigned!

HAUNTED HOUSE

A drab old house on the meadow
  Seen from the train;
Its color eaten by sunlight,
  Its years washed in by the rain.

In the tarnished dusk it stands there,
  Emptied of all delight;
Its windows, like eyeless sockets,
  Stare on an endless night.

Suddenly one raw sunbeam
  Writhes like a thing in pain,
And the eyes of that grim house sparkle—
  And go dead again.

WORDS FOR A JIG

(To be danced on the grave of an enemy)

Thus I pay the visit
  Promised years ago.
Tell me, loyal friend, how is it
  There below?

Do these weeds and mullein
  Choke each angry mood,
Or increase your hard and sullen
  Torpitude?

You who sought distractions
  Howsoever base,
Have you learned to love inaction's
  Slower pace?

Here, at least, you've found that
  You belong to earth;
Dying on the careless ground that
  Gave you birth.

Do not let it fret you;
  Things are not so drear.
Though the heartless world forget you,
  I am here!

I have not forgotten
  How you loved the stir;
Black at heart and doubly rotten
  Though you are.

So I take my fiddle,
  And I roar a stave;
Dancing gaily on the middle
  Of your grave.

And I tramp the new wood,
  And I shout halloo—
All the lively things that you would
  Like to do.

Such regard must cheer you
  In your misery,
Although I can scarcely hear you
  Thanking me.

But I ask no hands in
  Thanks or loud applause;
I am glad to sing and dance in
  Such a cause.

Thus I pay the visit
  Promised years ago. . . .
Tell me, loyal friend, how is it
  There below?

NIGHTMARE

It was cold that night by the lake,
  Something, I knew, was wrong
Though I whistled and tried to make
  The ends of a broken song.

Our footsteps crunched like a bite
  On leaves where the frost was strewn;
There was something false in the light
  Of that tarnished disc of a moon.

Like a rusty shield it hung
  Over a freezing abyss,
Cold as my heart, when you clung
  And stabbed me there with a kiss.

Then it grew light. I saw ships
  Huddling with frozen spars,
Your tell-tale eyes and your lips,
  And a sky that was stabbed with stars.

HABIT

Whatever may be false, let us agree
This much is true:
You have no magic left for me,
I wake no thrill in you.

You never speak of it, and yet I know
The tale is told;
Your kiss is plainer than a blow,
Too casual to be cold.

Well, let our yawning passion end unmarred
By all that's mean;
There is no thing so base and hard
As love's enforced routine.

END OF THE COMEDY

Eleven o'clock, and the curtain falls.
The cold wind tears the strands of illusion;
The delicate music is lost
In the blare of home-going crowds
And a midnight paper.

The night has grown martial;
It meets us with blows and disaster.
Even the stars have turned shrapnel,
Fixed in silent explosions.
And here at our door
The moonlight is laid,
Like a drawn sword.

THE WORN STRING

The weeks go past, the months slip by,
  The magic mood has lost its thrill.
And what, I wonder, is the tie
    That holds me still.

My eyes, cleared of the glamour, see
  You are not whimsical or wild;
A spirit footloose but not free,
    Childish, yet not a child.

On the soft airs of life you float,
  A butterfly with lazy wings;
Too purposeless to heed or note
    Ominous things.

Impervious to every taunt
  You dream and drift; you will not set
Yourself to win the things you want.
    You sink—and yet . . .

Yet I must make you glad and long
  For things you only half divine;
You are not great, you are not strong,
    But you are mine.

THE UNFINISHED PARTING

Why did she come? It would have been much
better
Had she but stayed away.
How could I hurt her then and let her
Hear what I had to say.

She came and sat there huddled, white and silent;
Not even daring to speak.
Against that mood I knew my violent
Words would be cruel and weak.

She had her best dress on, that cheap and flimsy
Affair of ribbons and tags.
It seemed a sort of pride or whimsy,
Like a ship going down with flags.

She knew we were to part there without quarrel-
ing;
She nodded while I spoke,
And bravely smiled till I said "Darling"—
And then she quivered and broke.

Sharper than strength and stronger far than duty,
I felt her silence press
The claim that held me, more than faith or beauty:
Her helplessness.

THE LAST DAY

I never thought our love could be so much
  More than the passion we could not resist,
Until the end, when you turned back to touch
  That rusty bench where first we sat and kissed.

I never saw the cruel world so fair,
  Nor knew how fast youth's bit of flame must die,
Until I saw you standing silent there
  With your young face against that wrinkled sky.

THE PARK REVISITED

This is the place; here is the tiny gap
Left in the hedge through which we tried to squeeze.
And here's the stretch of mall, that soft green lap
We entered shyly, guarded by the trees.

These are the same black twigs with their strange growth
Of brilliant yellow buds, that seem as though
They held all last year's sun. And here we both
Paused where the path ran off, and let it go.

A moment, I remember, you stood still,
Facing me glowing and yet gravely there—
And then you stumbled, laughing, up the hill,
Shaking down all your tossed and yellow hair.

I caught you at the top and, as we hung
Above the world, you trembled to the tips
Of your cool fingers. Then you turned and clung,
No longer frightened, to my arms and lips.

In what a torrent of imperative gladness
  Love swept us there; with what a reckless glow
We laughed at things like Time. . . . And was
    this madness
  In these prim walks less than a year ago?

FAIRMOUNT CEMETERY

Of all the nooks discovered,
  I like our first love best;
That screened-off bit of hillside,
  A soft, green nest.

A stream uncoiled beyond us;
  Trees shook their smoky plumes;
And, like a still procession,
  Marched the white tombs.

How often we would come there
  To love and talk of love;
The cemetery below us,
  Your heaven above.

And do you still remember
  The solemn pledge we tried
To write in blood and could not?
  And how you cried?

And how I dared the future
  With many a pompous speech?
" What," I stormed, " can touch us
  Whom death cannot reach!

" Pain shall drop his dagger;
  Care shall avert his face;
Defeated years shall triumph
  In our embrace!

" Rapt as two young conquerors,
  We shall laugh and know
Life is all that matters.
  We have made it so.

" Life is all that matters;
  Love is all that saves " . . .
Then I heard the dead men
  Chuckling in their graves.

AFTER A YEAR

There was a morning fresh with laughing
airs,
A sudden city-full of dancing feet;
And you came swiftly up the casual street,
Turning the landings into golden stairs . . .
I have forgotten it.

There was an afternoon we met and lied,
Evading every claim with counter-claim.
Fearing at last to call love by its name,
We stopped. And then you turned to me and
cried . . .
I have forgotten it.

There was an evening after torturing drouth,
With long hot silences and words ill-spent;
Suddenly your hurt eyes turned eloquent
And your cool lips lay quiet on my mouth . . .
I have forgotten it.

There was a night—I hear your white voice yet
Cleaving us as we hung there, heart to heart,
" Come, let us kiss and part as friends would
part,
And grieve a month or two, and so forget " . . .
Have *you* forgotten?

RETROSPECT

Why should this down-at-heels December day
  Remind me of the springs we knew together,
Of your thin hands and the peculiar way
  You had of looking back, hard to tell whether
    The eyes were solemn or gay?

It's raining, a slow, penetrating rain,
  Ending an afternoon of heavy languor.
And, like a trumpet-blast or a gust of pain,
  Comes your young face, flushed with a queer anger,
    Trying too hard to explain.

Trying to sound a note you could never find;
  Struggling to reach the depths of a puzzling emotion;
Groping among strange passions, bewildered and blind . . .
  Dear, how I envied that dogged devotion—
    All heart and no mind!

The strained assurance, the hysterical vow
  That silence, war or death could never sunder
Our bonds, our faith, and so on. . . . Yet somehow
  Those words persist, and this cold day I wonder
    Who hears them now.

CHANGE

What tricky chance, I wonder, made us meet
  After these stubborn years. In what a daze
I saw you smile and pass me on the street,
  While I stood staring at your altered face.

Where were those lights that woke a restless magic
  And leaped to find a swift and answering gleam?
Where the inscrutable eyes, the dark and tragic
  Lashes that drove me on from dream to dream?

Where were those mobile features? Where the lips
  I liked to think were proud, with just a strain
Of Eastern cruelty. . . . The glamour slips . . .
  You have grown soft and common, pink and plain.

What right had you to change! You come to
wake
Questions instead of clamorings in me.
Could I have been so blind, or did I make
You only what I wanted you to be?

And am I glad your presence left me cold?
Or do I wish, perhaps, I had been fired
With last year's flames? Can this be growing
old?
And am I wise this Spring, or merely tired?

DISILLUSION

The end is failure. Now the last
  Pretense goes down, a frayed disguise.
A cheap and folly-ridden past
  Is what I have to prize.

Sharper than all, the irony
  Of being caught in my own mesh;
The self-deceit that tried to be
  An exaltation of the flesh.

The grandiose emotions seem
  Ridiculously small and crass;
A fool's attempt to build a dream
  Lower than what he wants—and has.

Failure. Yet this I gain thereby:
  When my desires grow feverish,
At least they will not strain and try
  To find a goddess in a wish.

FREE

And suddenly the touch of flesh
  Is hateful as these hungry curves;
And every point of contact is a fresh
  Agony to these whipped and exhausted nerves.

Warm hollows, will you never let
  Me go till you have buried all my will?
Oh, to be free of the body, to lie and forget
  The use of lips and hands, to lie and be still.

I want a bed with room to spare,
  Where nothing breathes and sleep is sure;
There lust shall have a deeper sense, for there
  The worm shall be my only paramour.

Slowly the worm shall have his fill
  (As I have had) of flesh and frequency,
Until the body falls away, until
  Passion devours me—and sets me free.

GOLD AND WHITE

The snow on the yellow pavement;
    And the light of your coming—
Why should it make my cooled blood hot
    With a new drumming?

And my mind runs back to a windy meadow,
    Where the wind lays his
Breath on an agitated pool of buttercups
    With a froth of daisies.

Waves of yellow and white where a lavish tide
    Has flung them;
Tossed in a bright and futile abandon—
    And you among them. . . .

You stand, as you stood there, strangely unreal,
    Warm and quiescent.
Yet something eludes me; you melt like these
        snowflakes,
    Escaping the present.

SURRENDER

I have given myself to Life
Utterly.
Not knowing what she will do with me
Nor what thing, in the end, she will make me do.
She, the most proud and passionate mistress,
Shall laugh and possess me,
Calling, holding me close and carousing;
Filling the cups of my love
Till she knows I am sated.

And then—I shall leave her
Slowly, half-heartedly;
Turning from her warm side to a warmer breast.
Finding, at last, the long-sought and perfect,
Deep-eyed and patient
Mistress and mother.

THE PRODIGAL

Abashed and blundering I have come back
  To force the liberal bounty of your love;
To ask for what I never had to lack
    Or take too little of.

The brazen, desperate demands
  Are halted by your clouded eyes;
Your cooling and compassionate hands
    Choke my well-meaning lies.

Your wounded faith, your lavish love,
  The glittering heights I cannot reach,
Those bright nobilities reprove
    Me more than any speech.

Softly your silence, like an unrung bell,
  Breaks into gentle music, and the black
Barriers lift as, from a transient hell,
    I have come back.

THE CURE

"Heal me, beloved, and have me
  Strong at your side.
I am weak, I am cold and hungry
  For all that you have denied.
I shall die with loving a promise—
  Heal me! " he cried.

She put her hands on his forehead;
  She touched his lips and sighed.
With a warm and lavish abandon,
  She flung off her pride.
She healed him of his sickness,
  And it was she that died.

THE WISE WOMAN

His eyes grow hot, his words grow wild;
He swears to break the mold and leave her.
She smiles at him as at a child
That's touched with fever.

She smoothes his ruffled wings, she leans
To comfort, pamper and restore him;
And when he sulks or scowls, she preens
His feathers for him.

He hungers after stale regrets,
Nourished by what she offers gaily;
And all he thinks he never gets
She feeds him daily.

He lusts for freedom; cries how long
Must he be bound by what controlled him!
Yet he is glad the chains are strong,
And that they hold him.

She knows he feels all this, but she
Is far too wise to let him know it;
He needs to nurse the agony
That suits a poet.

He laughs to see her shape his life,
As she half-coaxes, half-commands him;
And groans it's hard to have a wife
Who understands him.

THE HOLY CITY

You are my holy city, my beloved;
  Dark as Jerusalem and bright as Rome.
The gates of you are opened generously
    To take the wanderer home.

What foreign towns I knew have never dimmed
  The burning memory of your altar-fire;
My backward-hungering heart has always heard
    In other songs, your choir.

I kiss your lips and dream of Lebanon!
  You are my living Zion: and I rest
Here in the temple of your body's grace,
    Beneath the white wall of your breast.

ESCAPE

When toil with many a promise
  Would keep me in its pay,
Her breast, it is my Sabbath,
  Her lips, my holiday.

I laugh at labor, knowing
  Its ineffectual power
Here, in her holy bosom's
  Serene and certain hour.

Here I am held and washed in
  Waves of a great content,
Tides of majestic passions
  That never can be spent.

Her arm is some white harbor
  Where ships can lie at peace,
And there church-bells are ringing
  And happy songs increase.

There I would end my journeys
  And never slip away—
Her breast, my singing Sabbath,
  Her lips, my holiday.

YOU

Is this your body that my fingers touch?
  And are these lips but lips, that can reveal
Splendor of marching skies,—so much
  More than the flesh can feel.

Under the savage heat and rude desire
  A sudden glory breaks, half-felt, half-seen;
I rise upon a sea of singing fire
  That lifts and sweeps me clean.

The rumble and the clash of war have gone
  Into my blood that shouts its battle-cry;
Even your beauty keeps me struggling on
  Toward that for which men die.

You hold me closely, yet you set me free
  For unknown struggles with a great release;
You are my red desire of victory
  And my white dream of peace.

HEREAFTER

When Time with its cruel abandon
  Treats all of our dreams with disdain,
Though he sweeps out the ashes of memory,
    Two things will remain.

Two things will persist through the darkness
  When Death reaches out for the rest:
Your flower-like hand on my forehead;
    My lips on your breast.

BIRTHDAY

Cleave the stubborn heart of me.
  Grapple and remove
This unbearable apathy—
  Rouse me with your love.

With the flint of loveliness,
  Strike my wooden pride;
Till, in flames, a hot excess
  Burns me to your side.

Rising from the coils of fire,
  Kindle this damp fuel.
Surge within me; blaze and . . .

No, no. This is not right. The words are false;
Even the tune is wrong.
Here I am fumbling with the annual song
That hesitates and halts

In cold repugnance at the lyric lies.
What are these cries
But cowardly appeals for you
To do what I should do;
Verbal mechanics built to shape
Means for a possible escape?

The lie, the pitiful irony of it all!

I, who have burned you out, turn and appeal
For greater warmth, new strength to feel
What I have squandered in impenitent greed . . .
And now I call
On you again to give me the one thing
That you most need!

Well, having started so to sing
Unworthily, at least I can be still.
And, having fed on you, I can begin to feed . . .
But what have I to offer? What can fill
The empty balance of my debt? This blood,
Brain and body I will break and make into
A sacrament worthy of the starved desire of you.
Yet that will never make it good.
The proffer of regenerated love?
It is not great enough.

Only one thing remains—
The will to make you care
For what lies almost buried in despair;
The faith that, struggling from its sordid chains,
Is its own prayer . . . .

Something has taken root in me—or do I grow
Because of it? No matter. This stays true,
This much at least I know:
Through me forgotten flames will rise to quicken
you
With an exalted glow.
Be glad, be glad that now it is my turn
To make you burn!

FULFILMENT

Here, at your delicate bosom, let death come
To me
Where night has made a warm Elysium
Lulled by a soft, invisible sea.

Now in the porches of your soul I stand
Where once I stood;
Fed and forgiven by a liberal hand,
My broken boyhood is renewed.

You are my bread and honey set among
A grove of spice;
An ever-brimming cup; a lyric sung
After the cannonade and battle-cries.

You are my well-loved earth, forever fresh,
Forever prodigal, forever fond;
As, from the sweet fulfilment of the flesh,
I reach beyond.

Printed in the United Kingdom
by Lightning Source UK Ltd.
119192UK00002B/81